FAIRIES & FRIENDS

ENCHANTING FAIRIES AND FRIENDS TO COLOR

BARBARA LANZA

Dedication

To Ed, Gina, Nick and Chris
with gratitude and admiration

Colored by

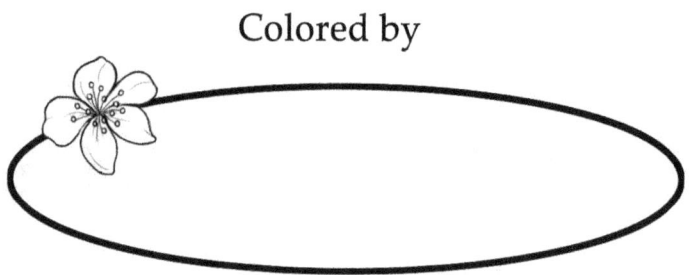

Fairies and Friends includes twenty-five never before published
pictures. Color more scenes of this serene world first introduced
in the coloring book, Fairy Lane.
The paper is not bleed proof, so please place a heavy piece of
paper under each page to be colored if using markers, etc.
It is hoped coloring this world adds more seenity to yours.

Barbara

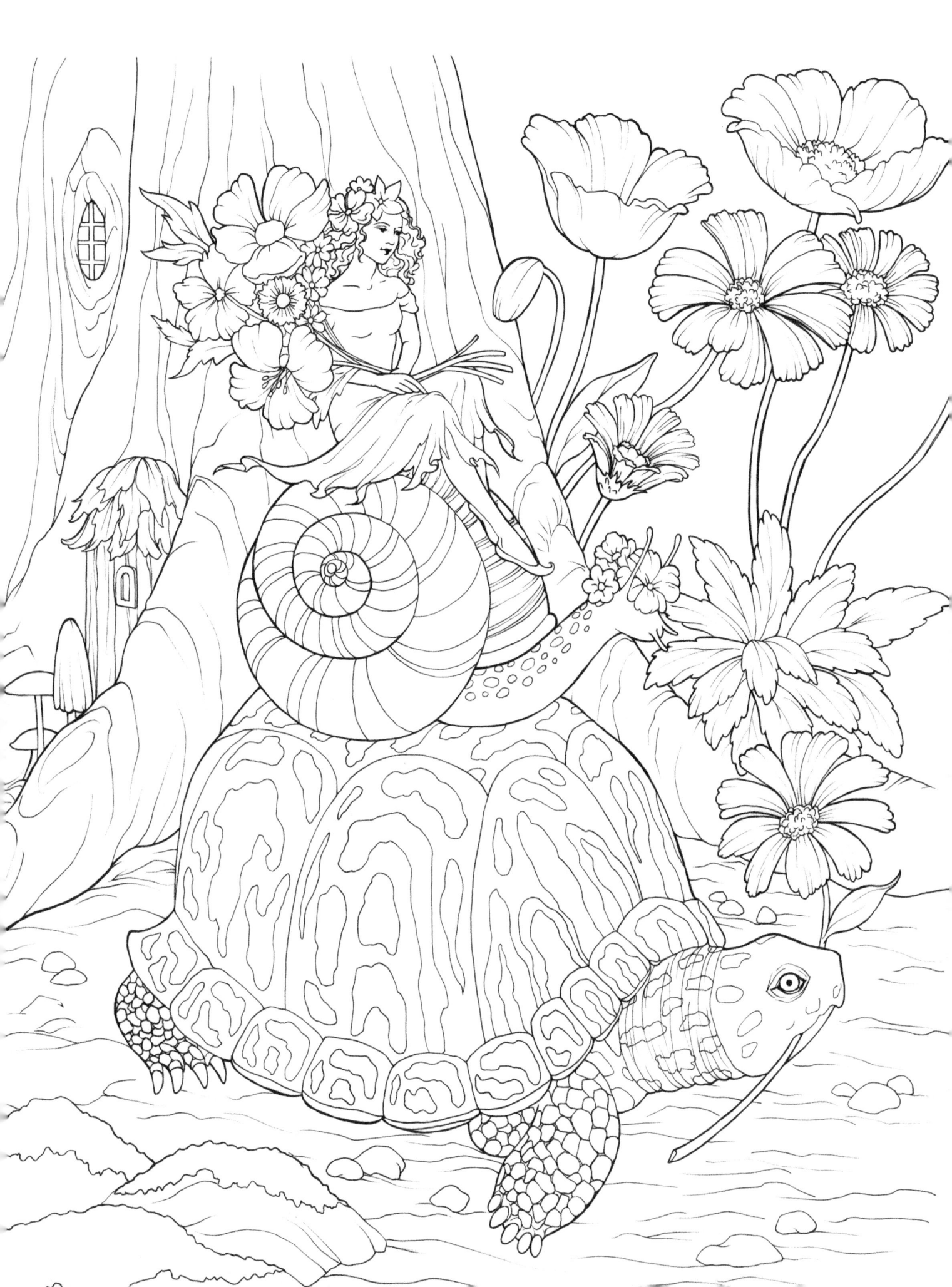

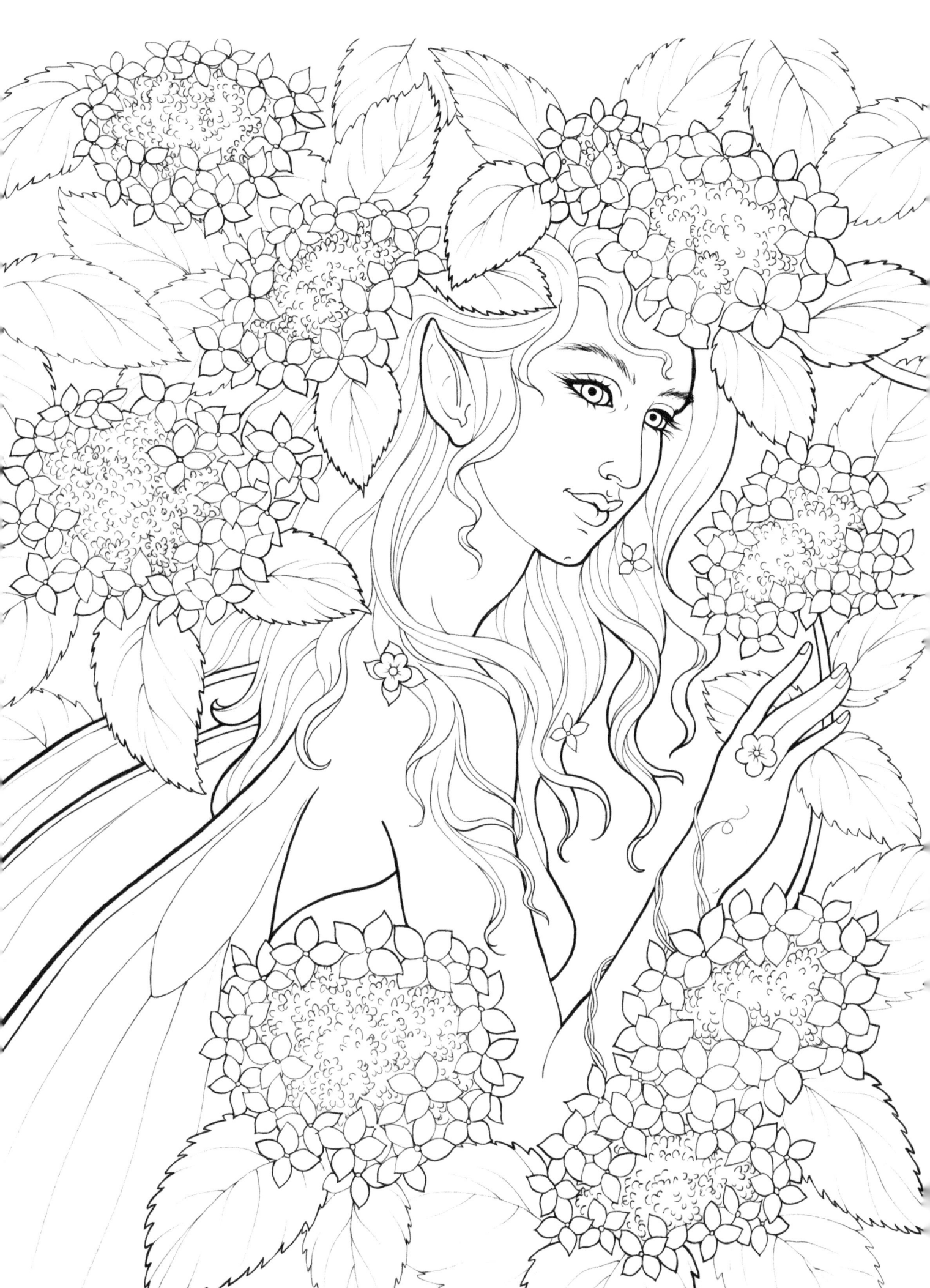

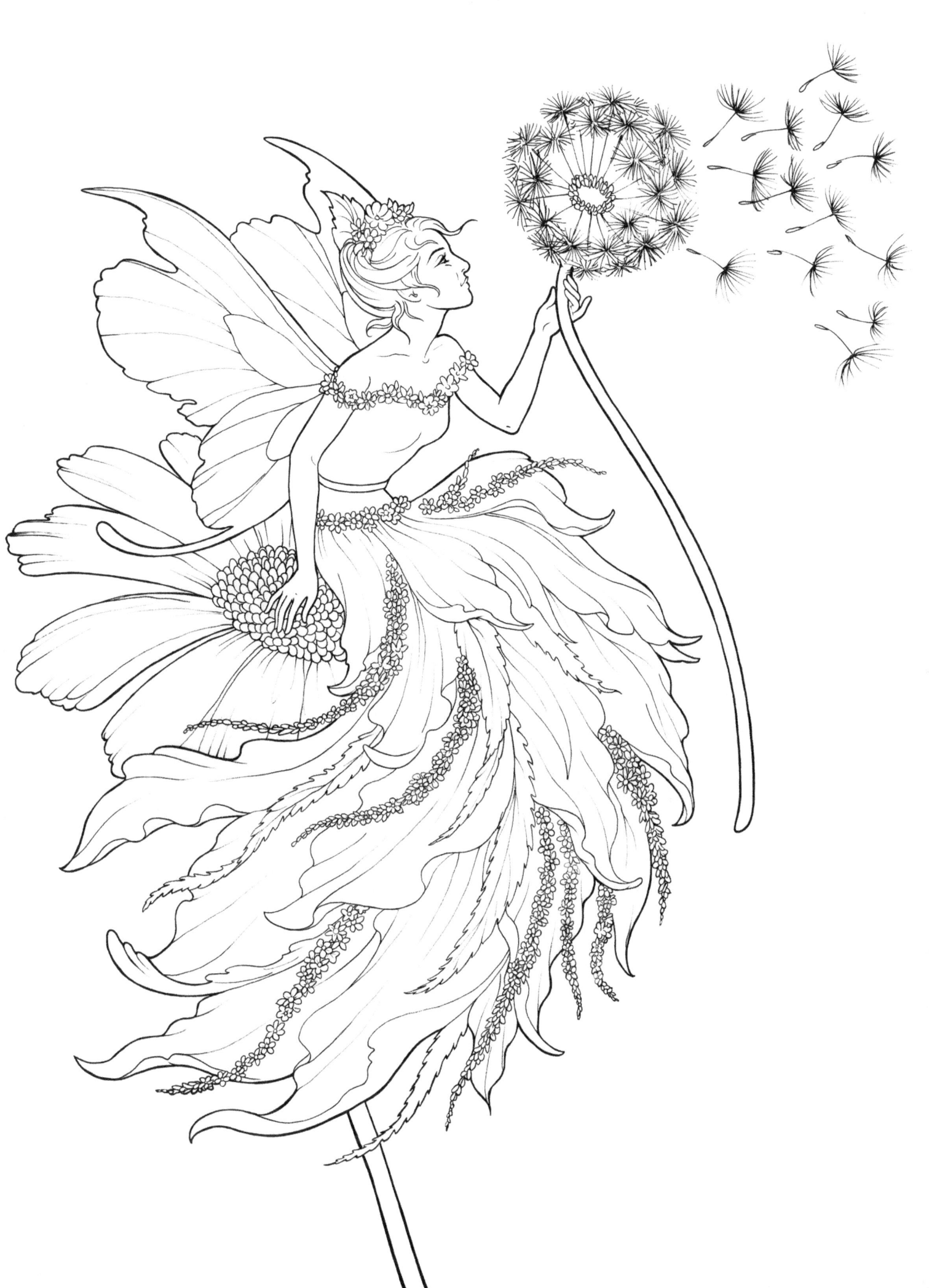

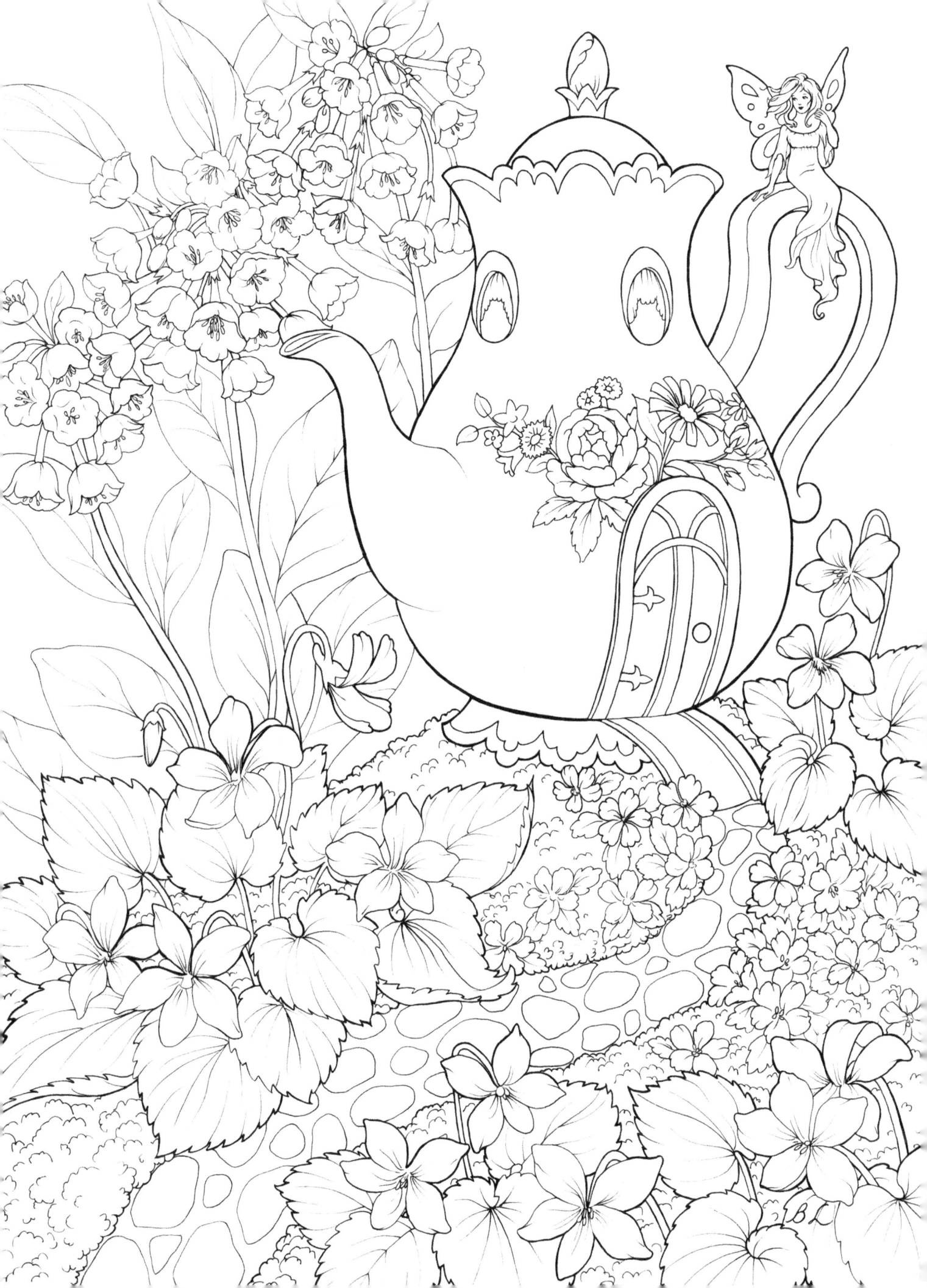

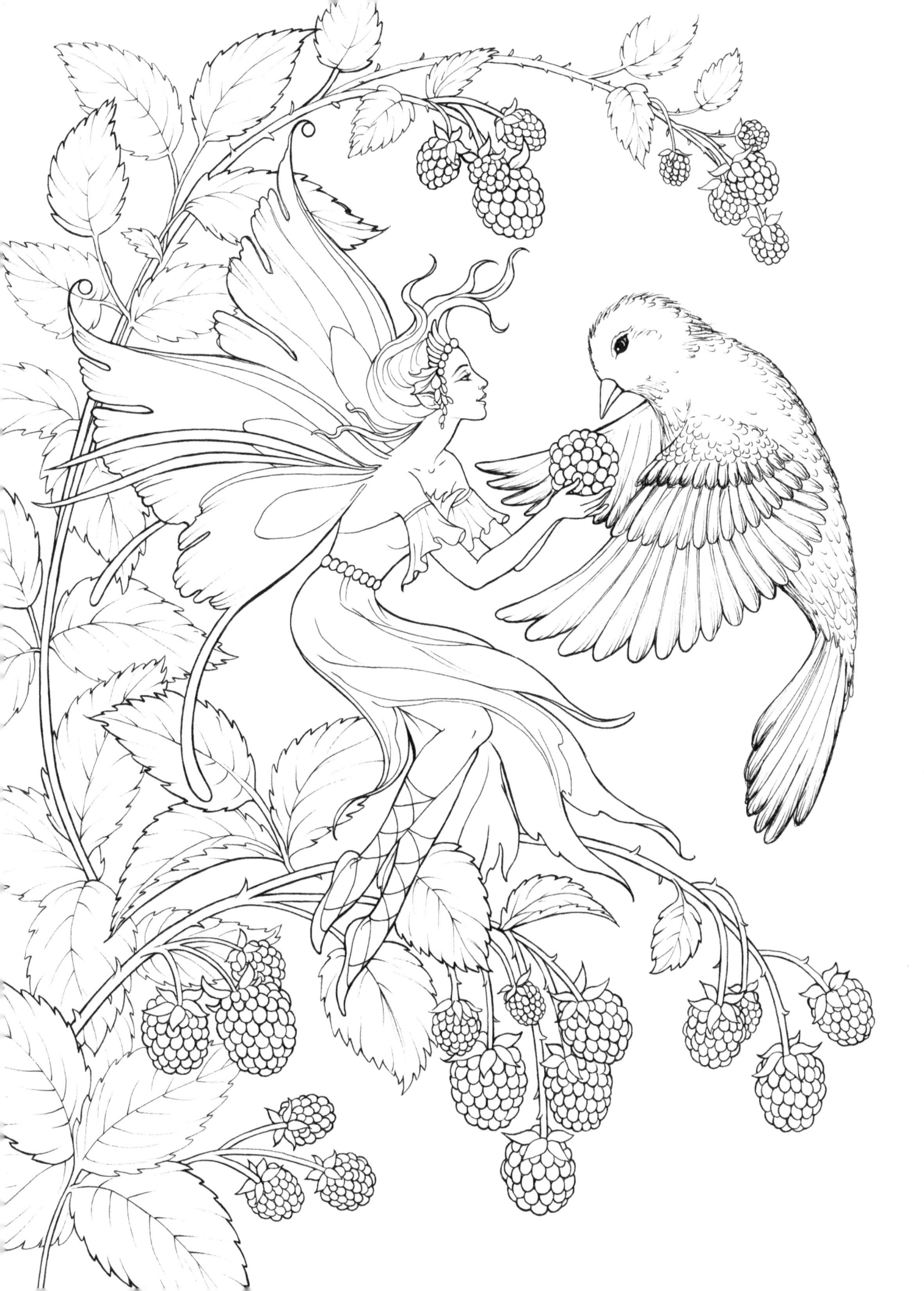

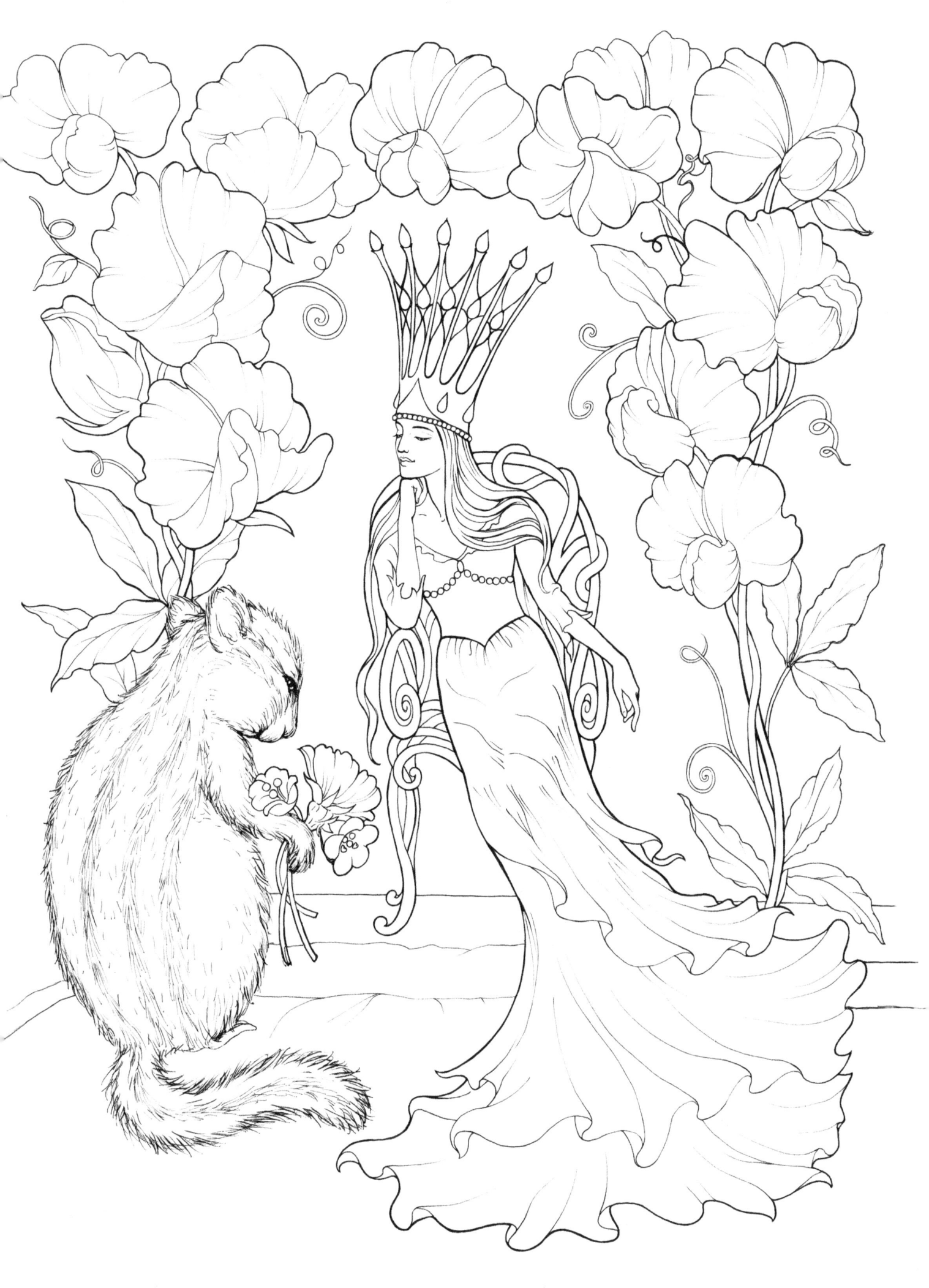

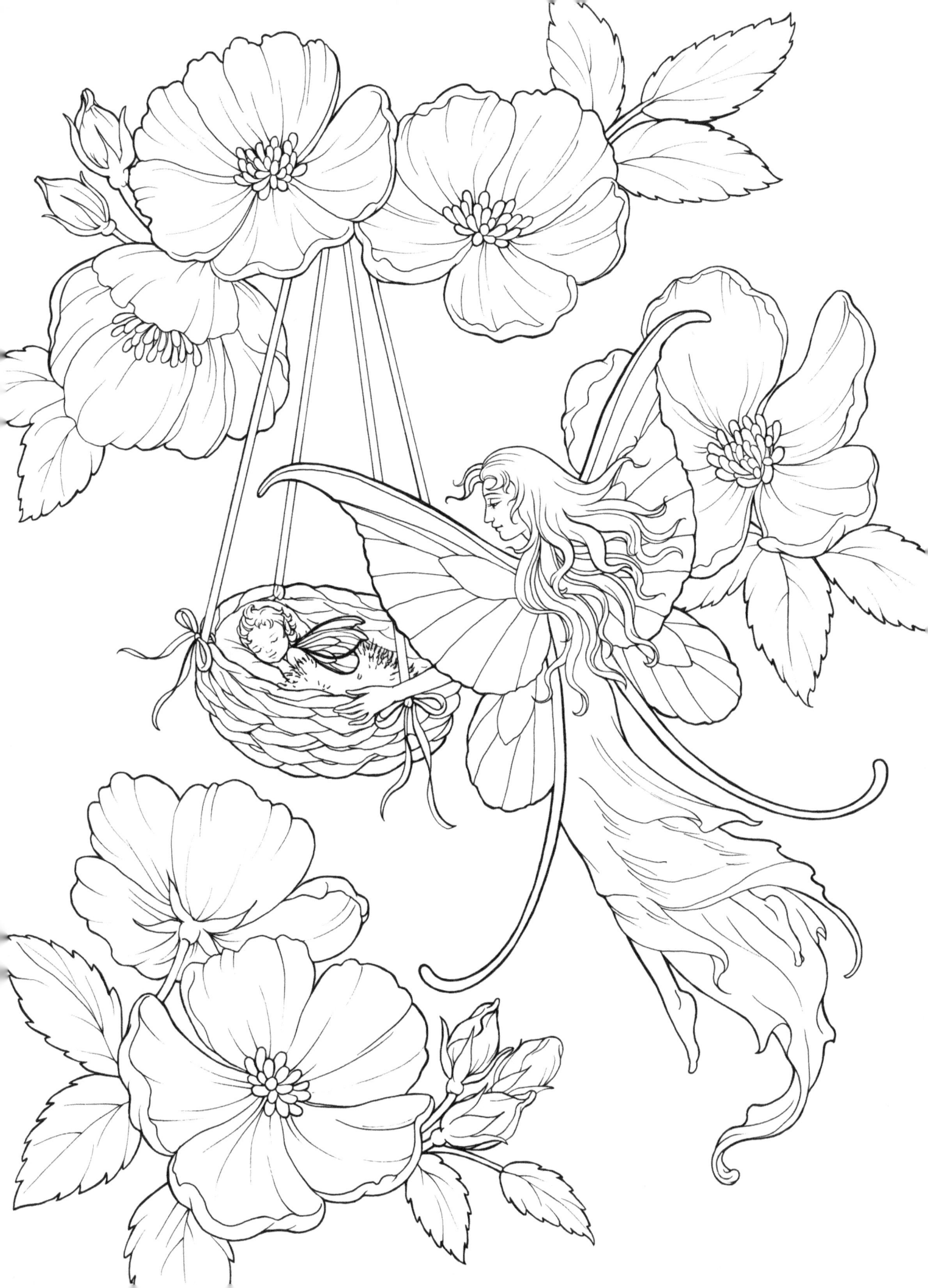

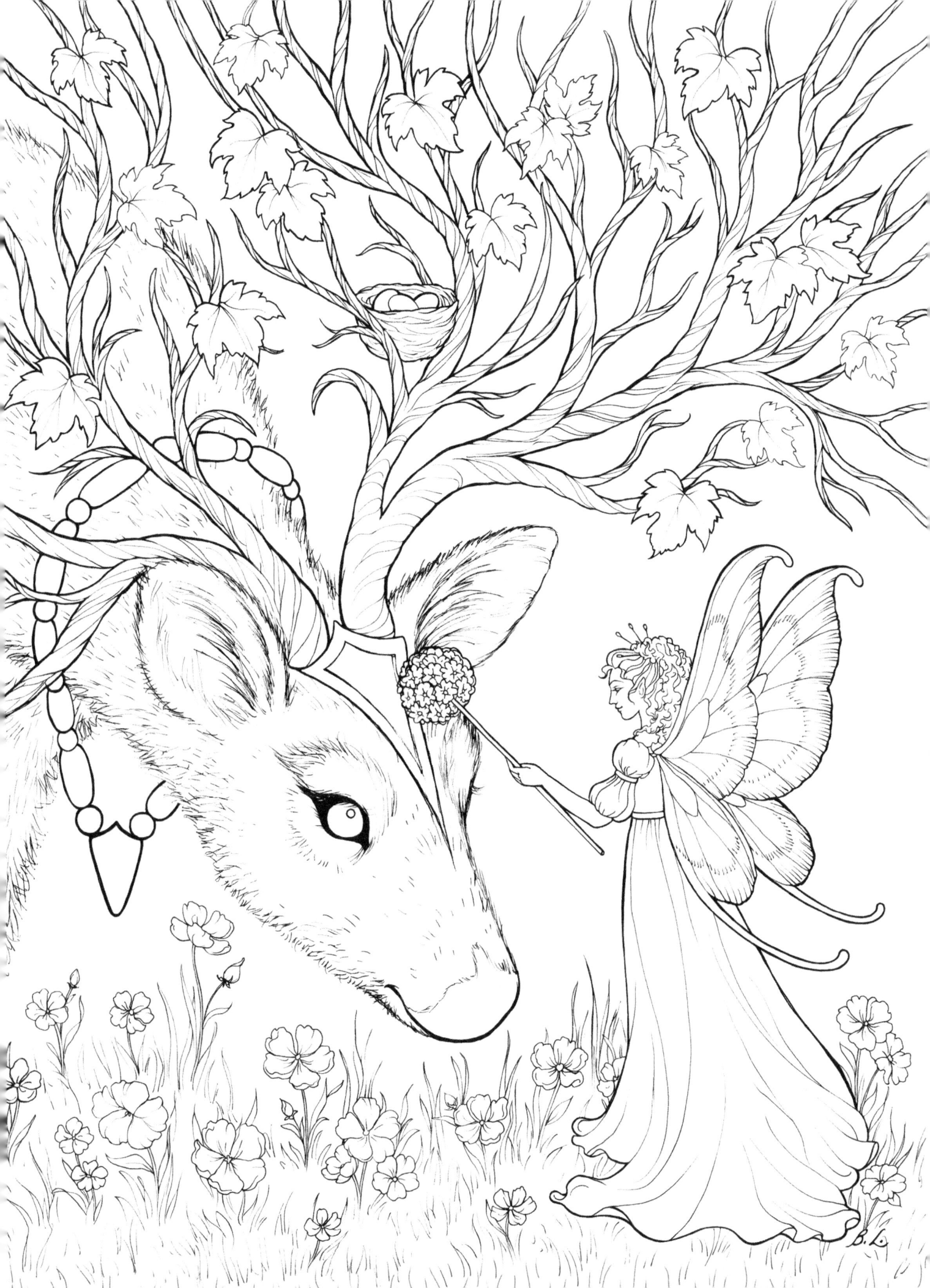

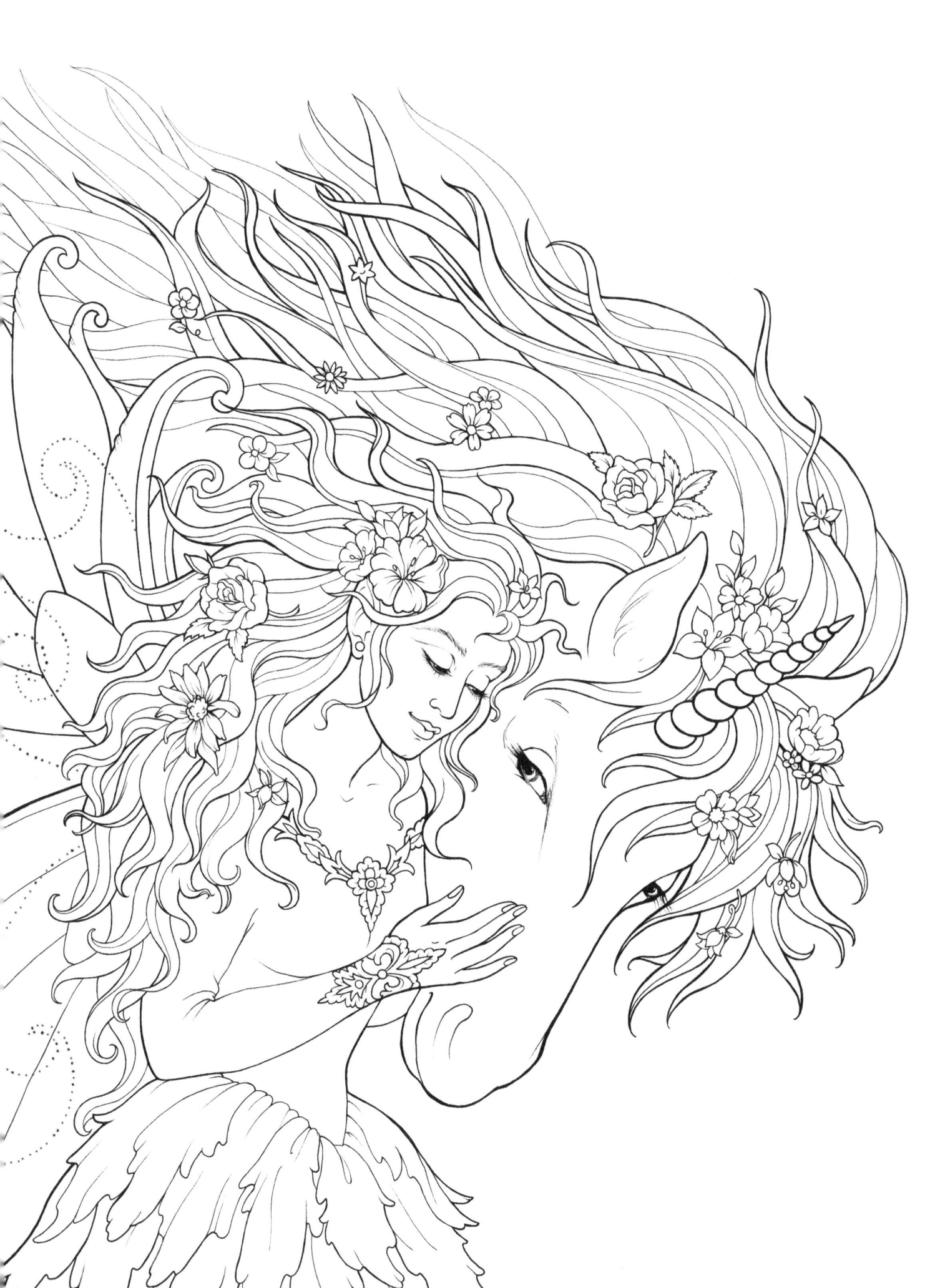

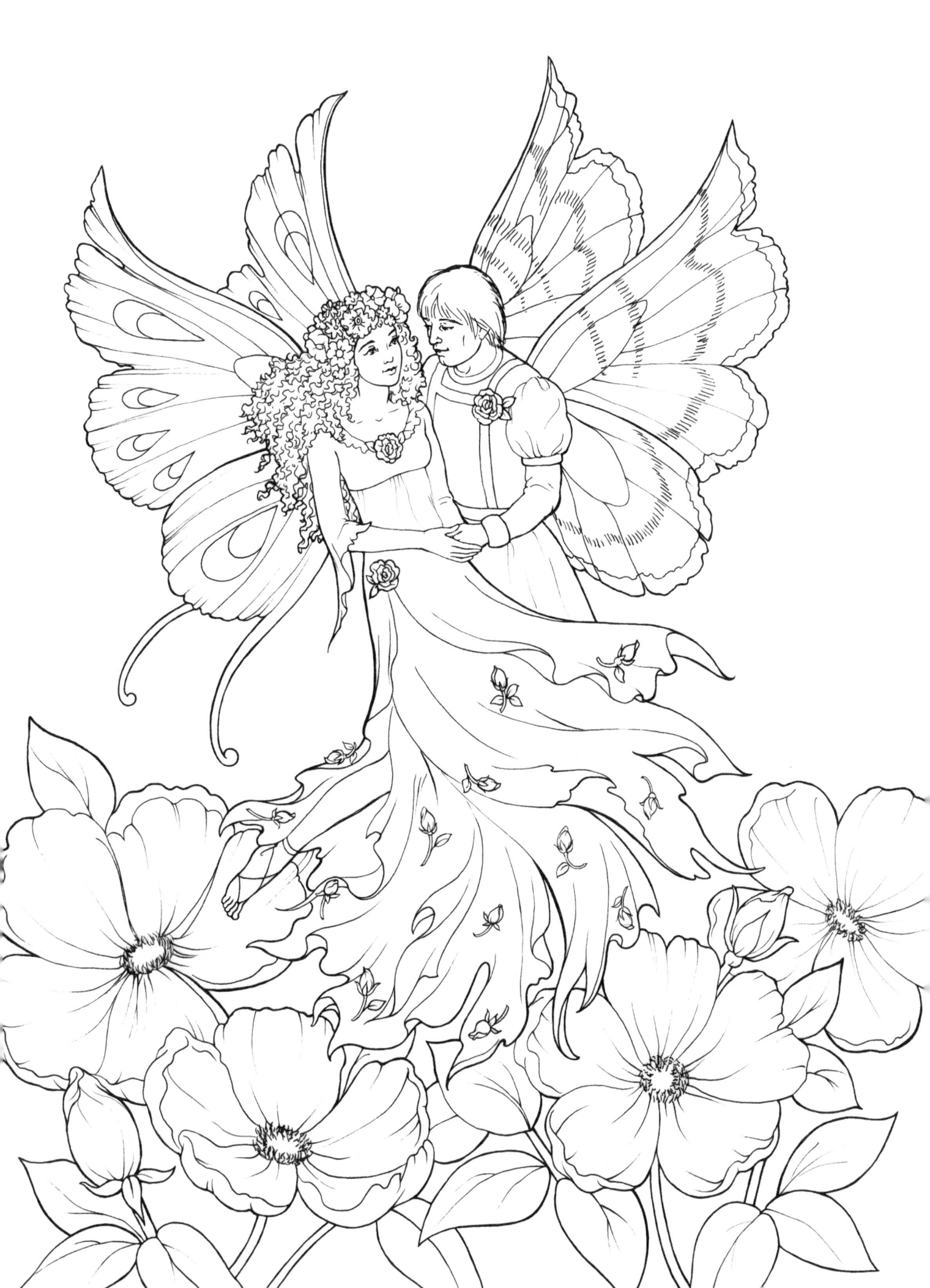

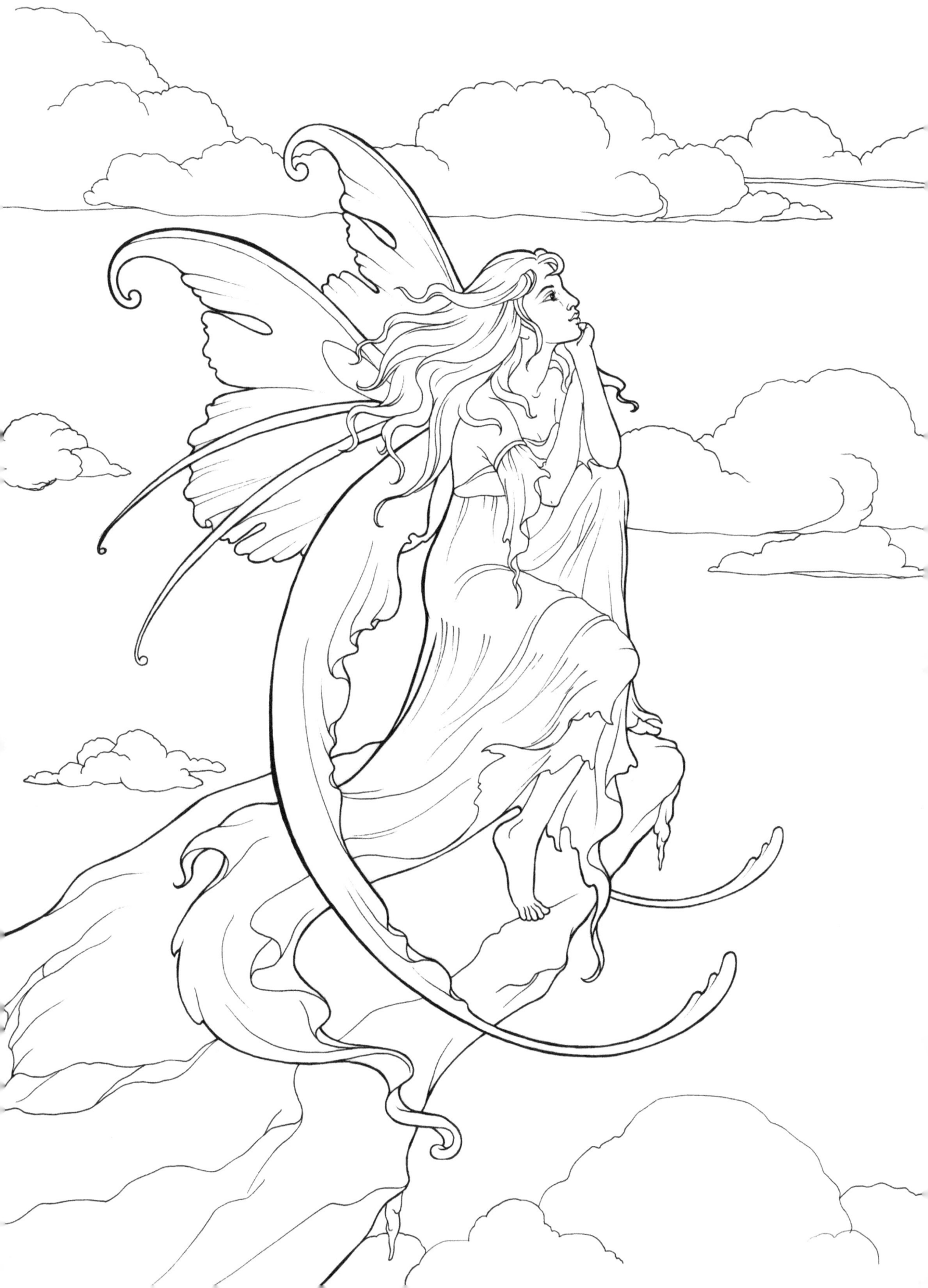

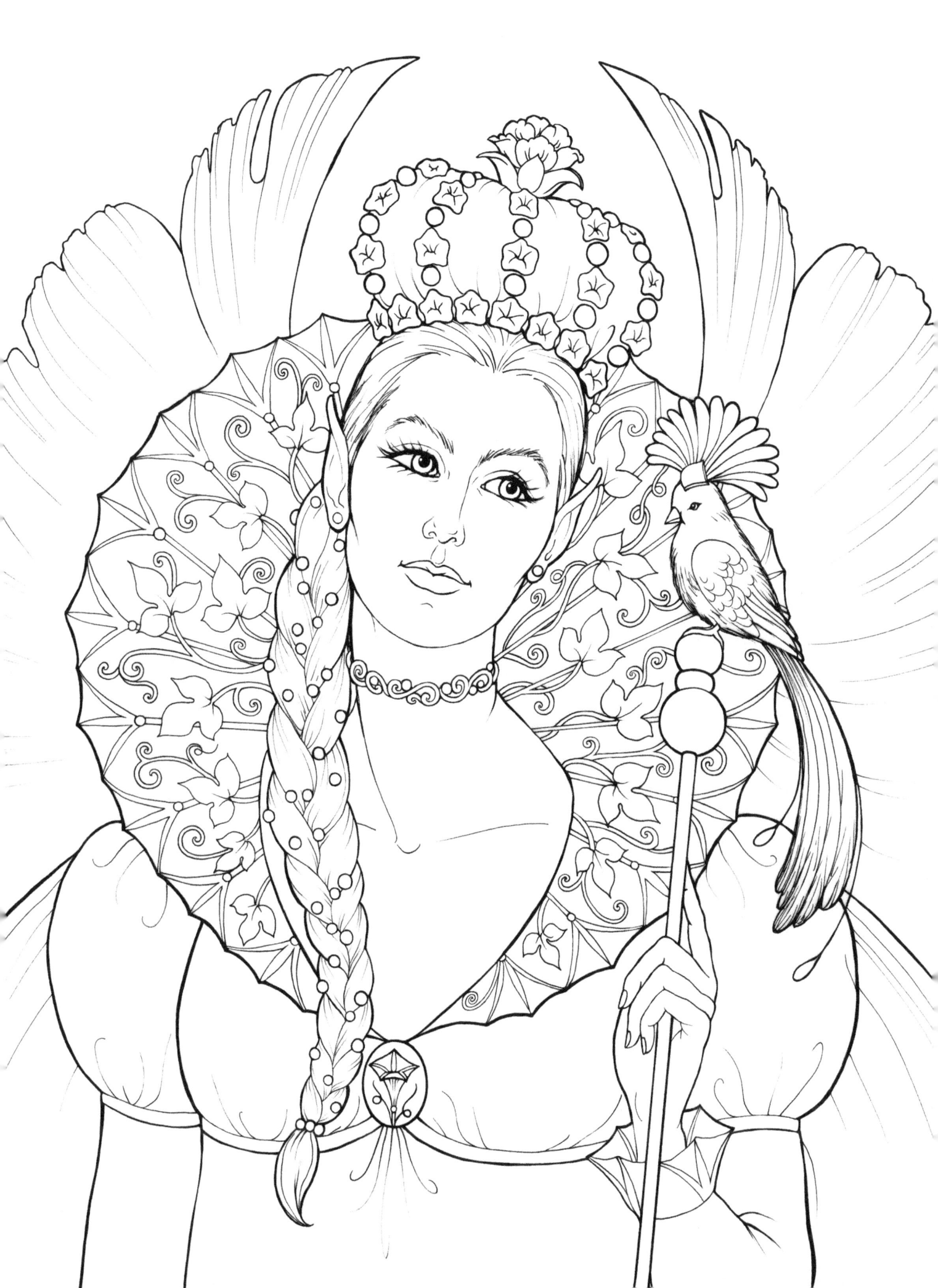

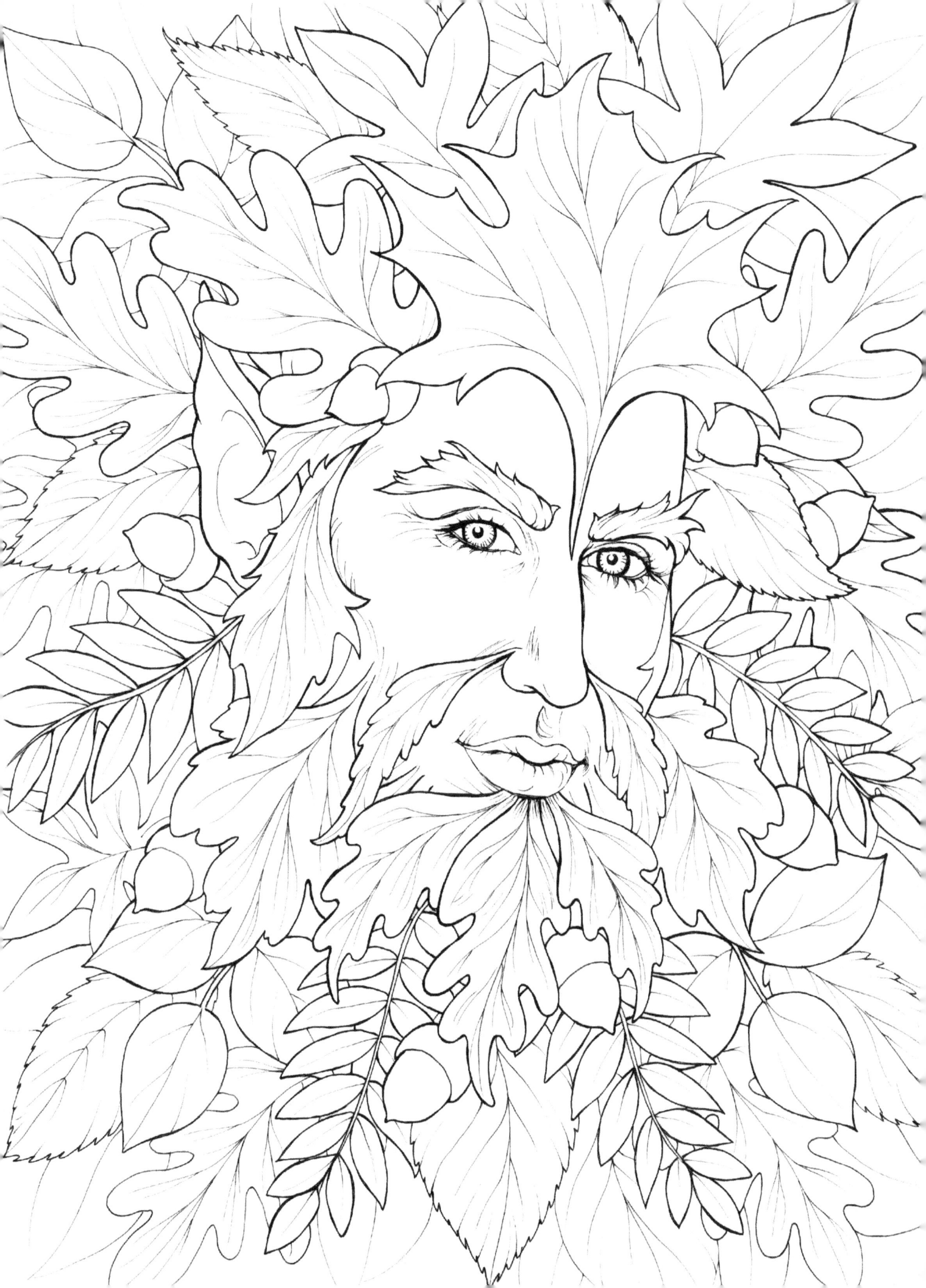

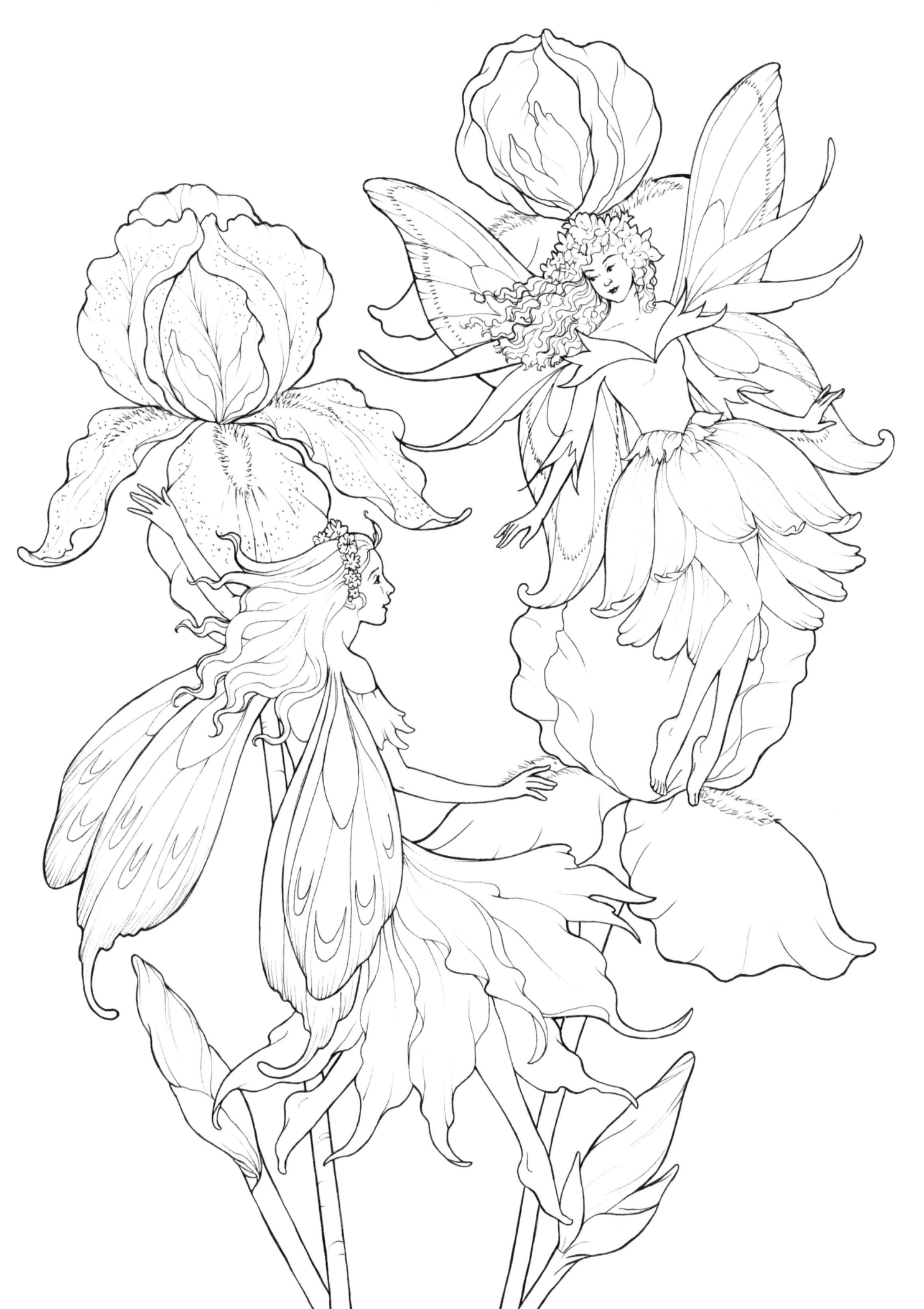

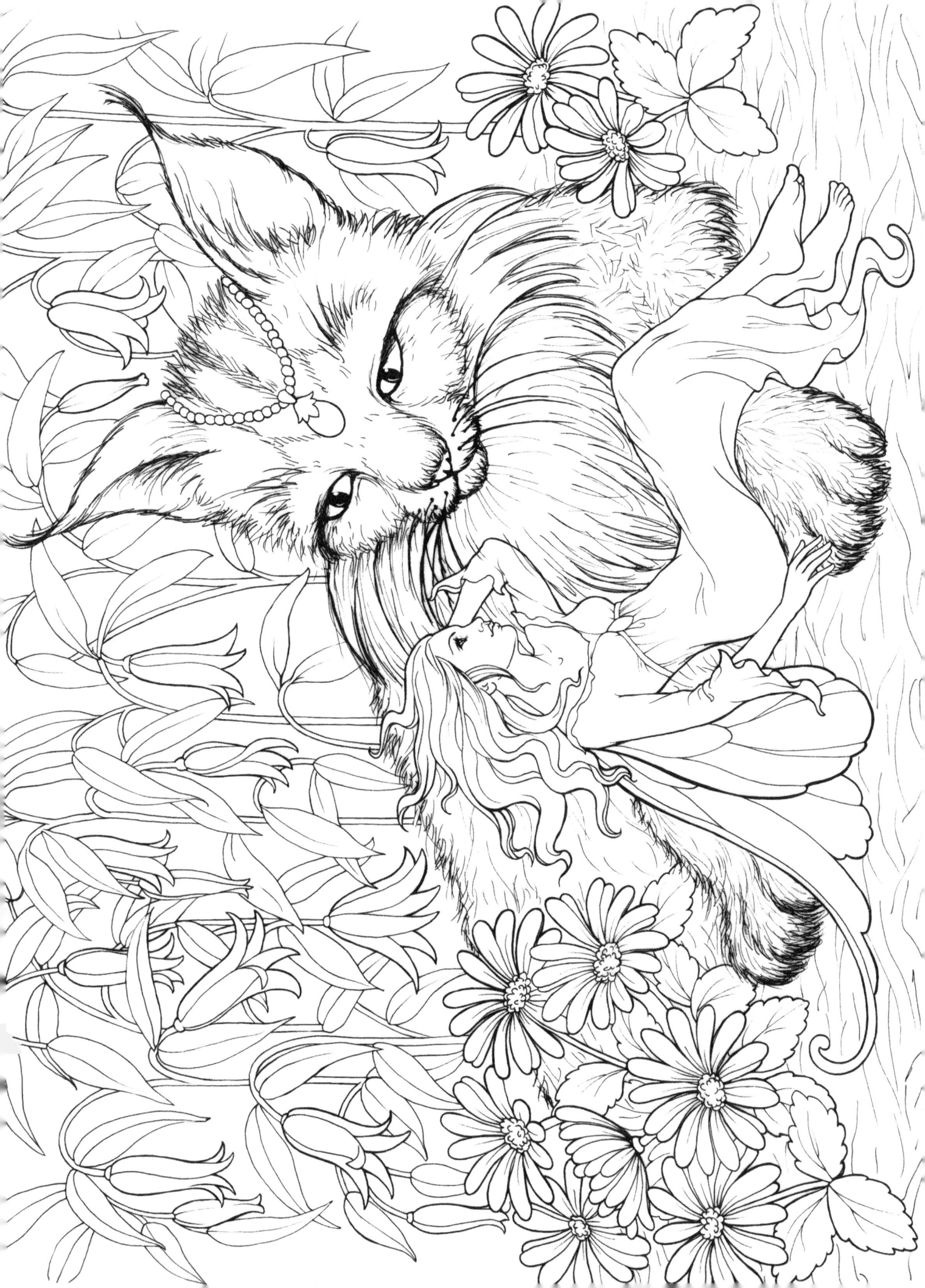

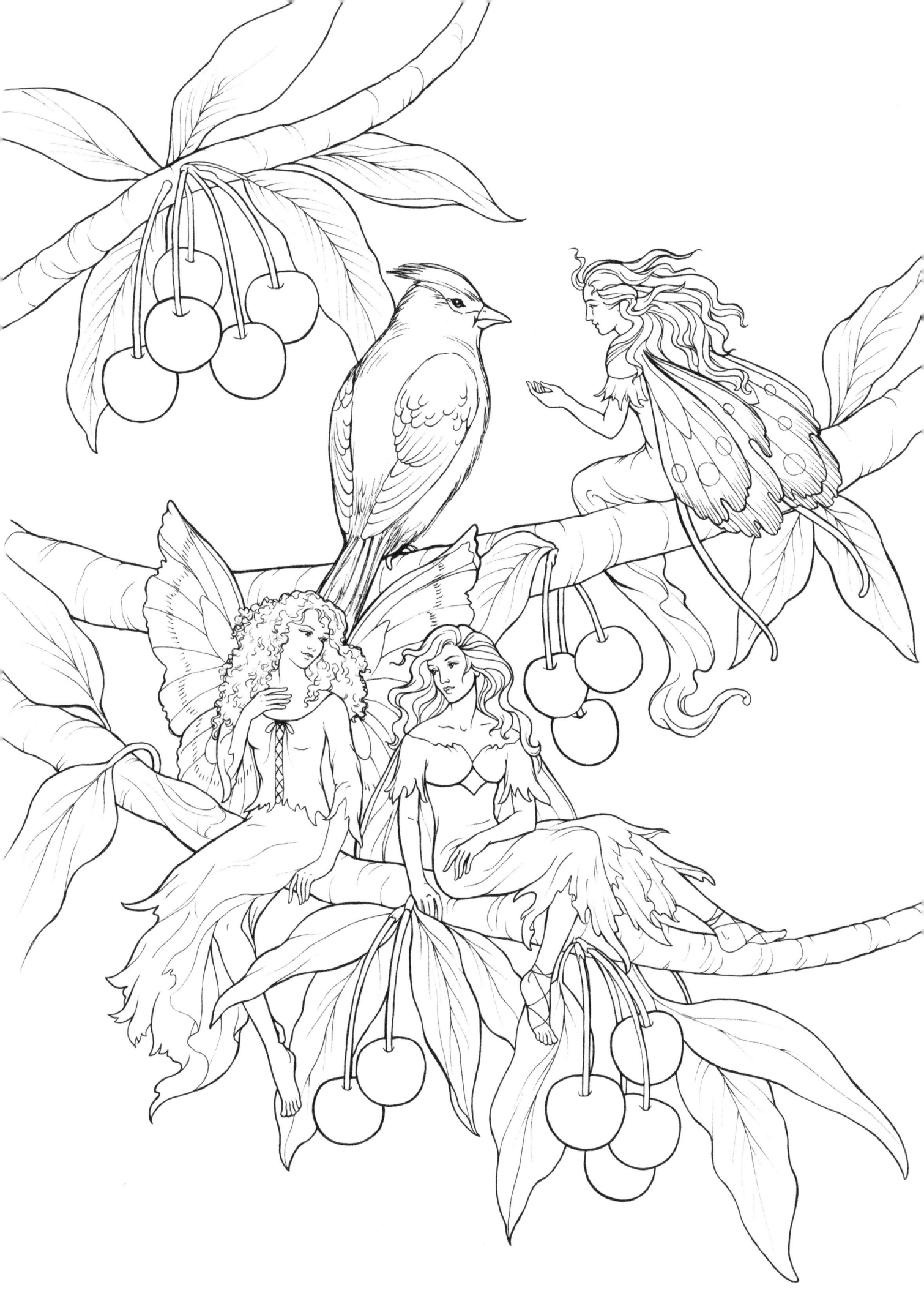

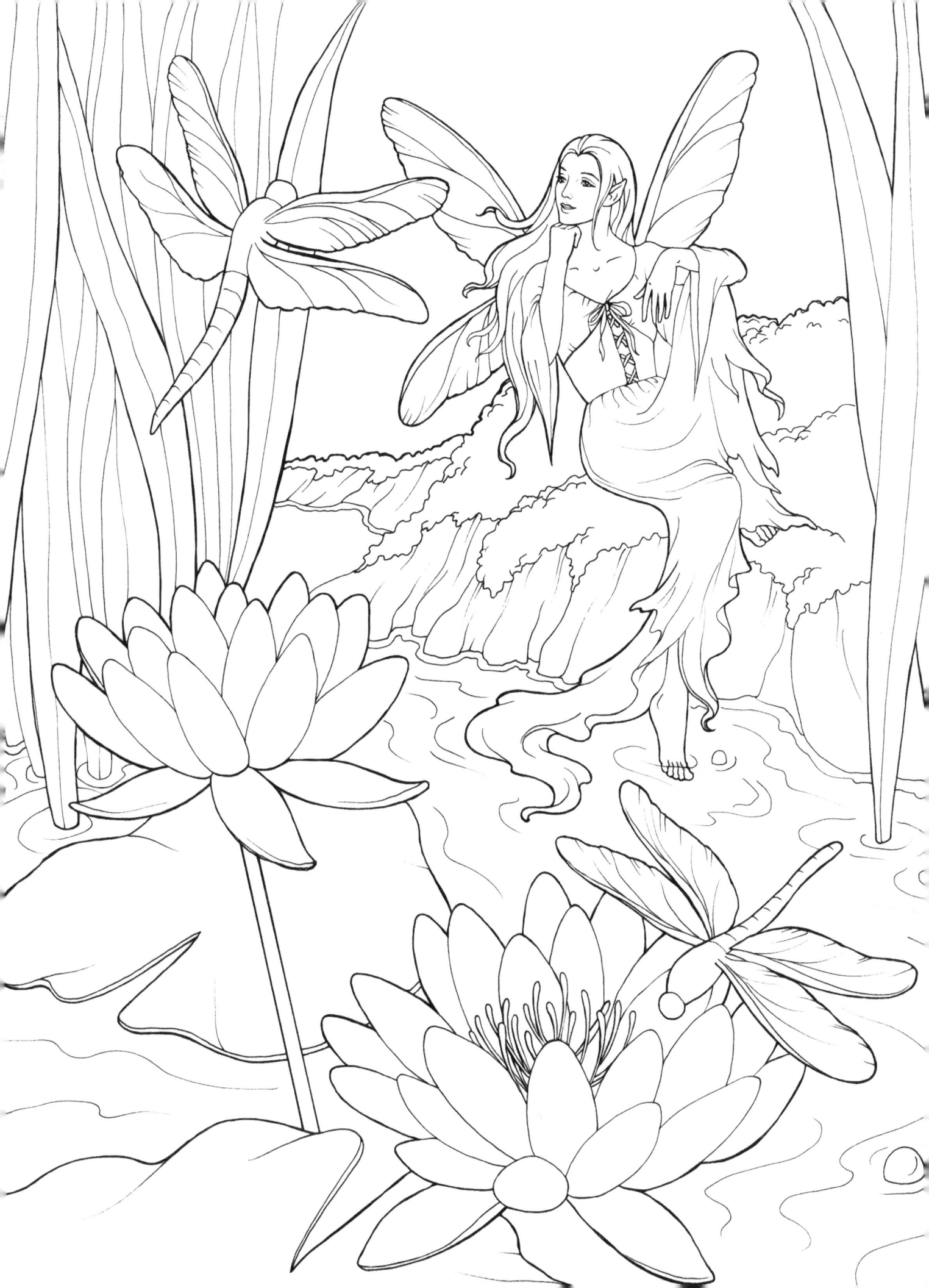

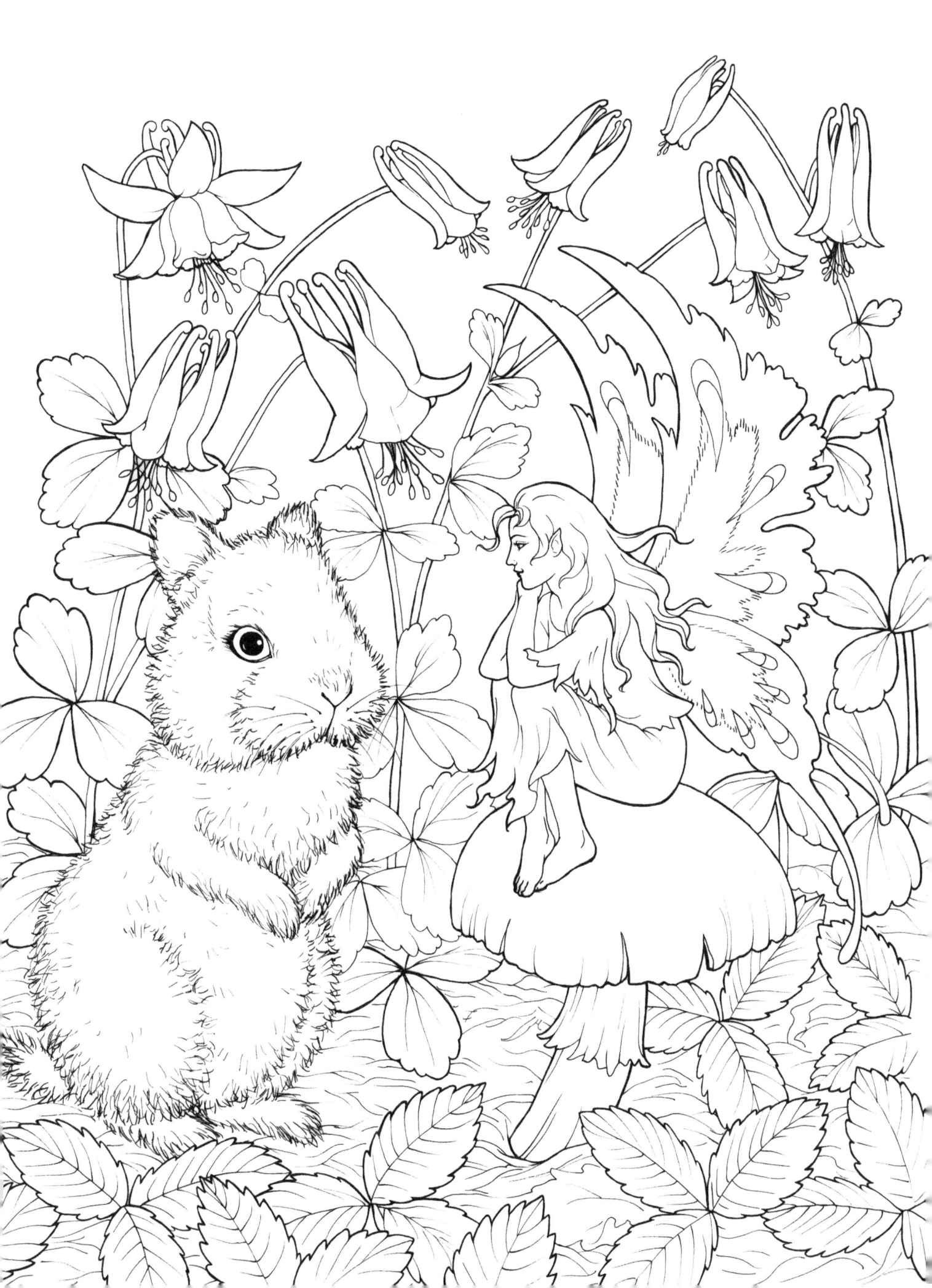

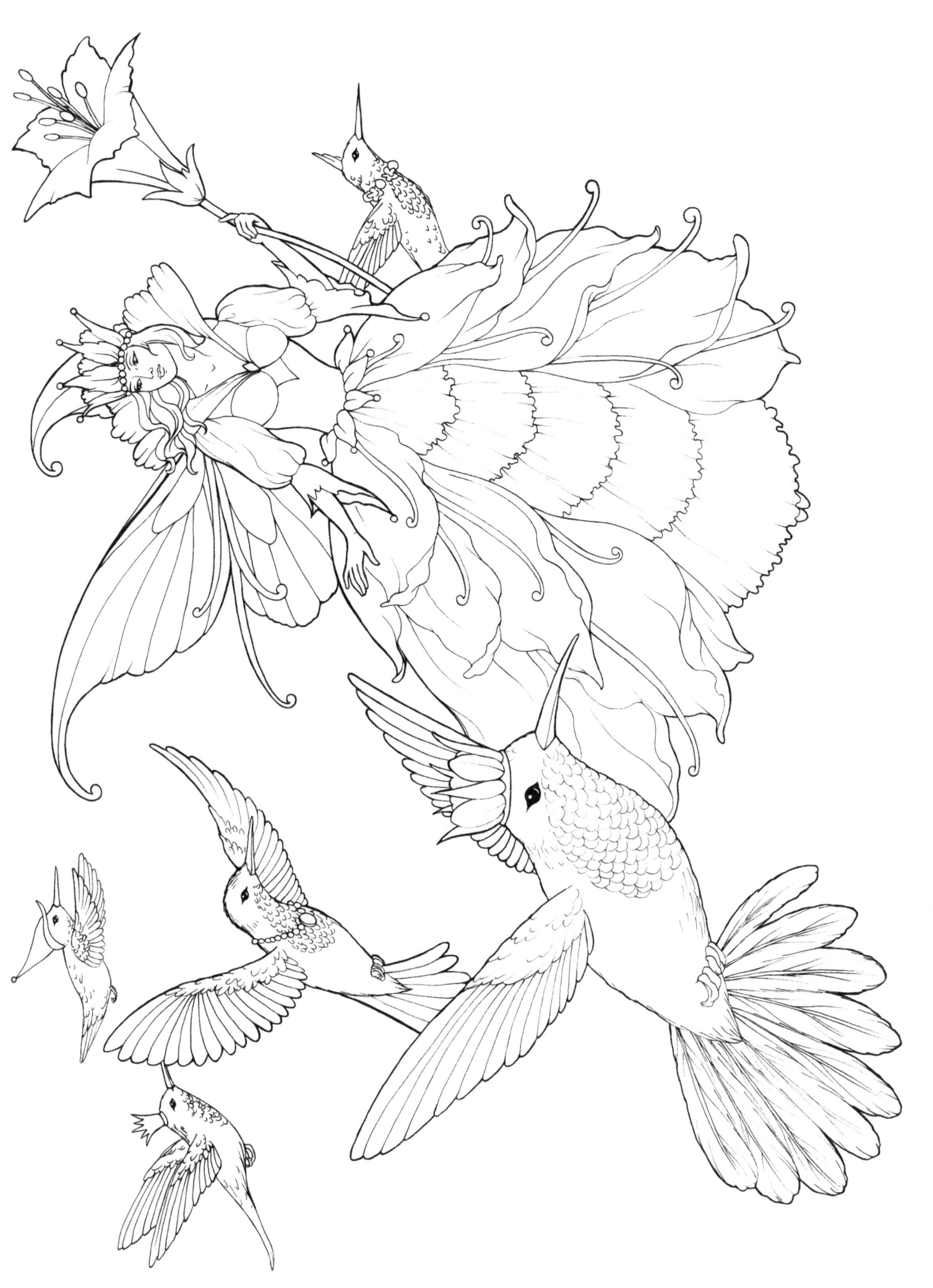

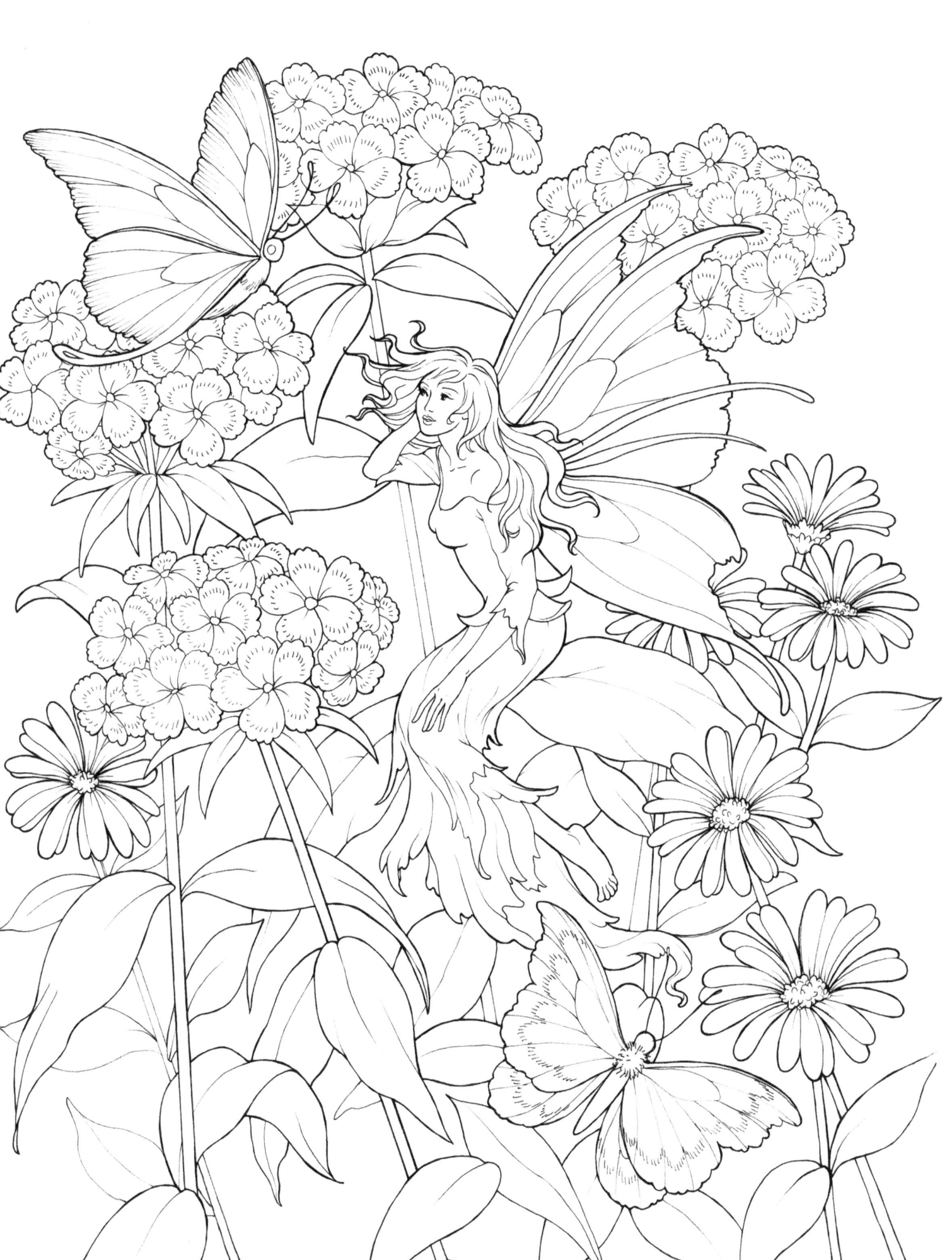

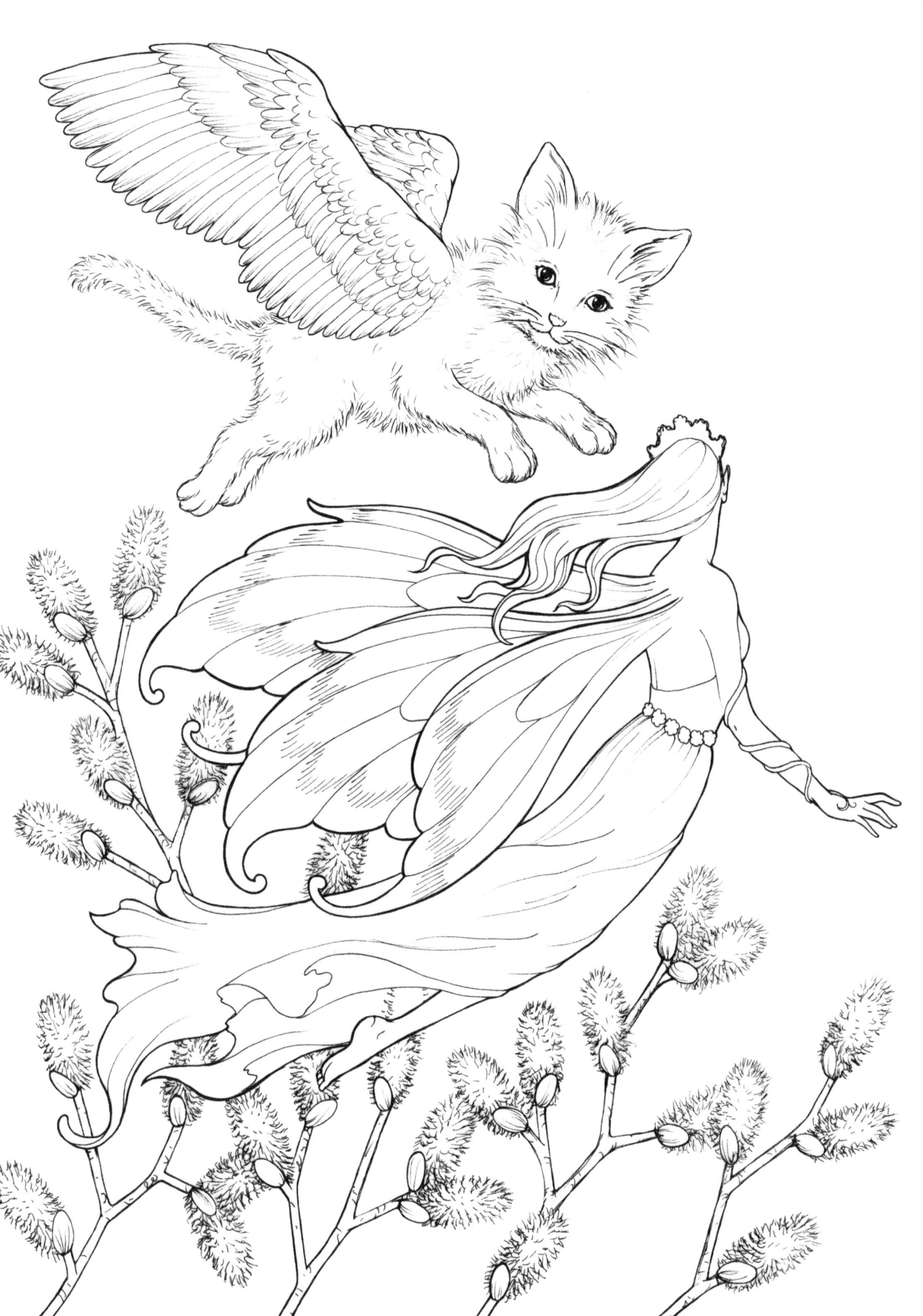

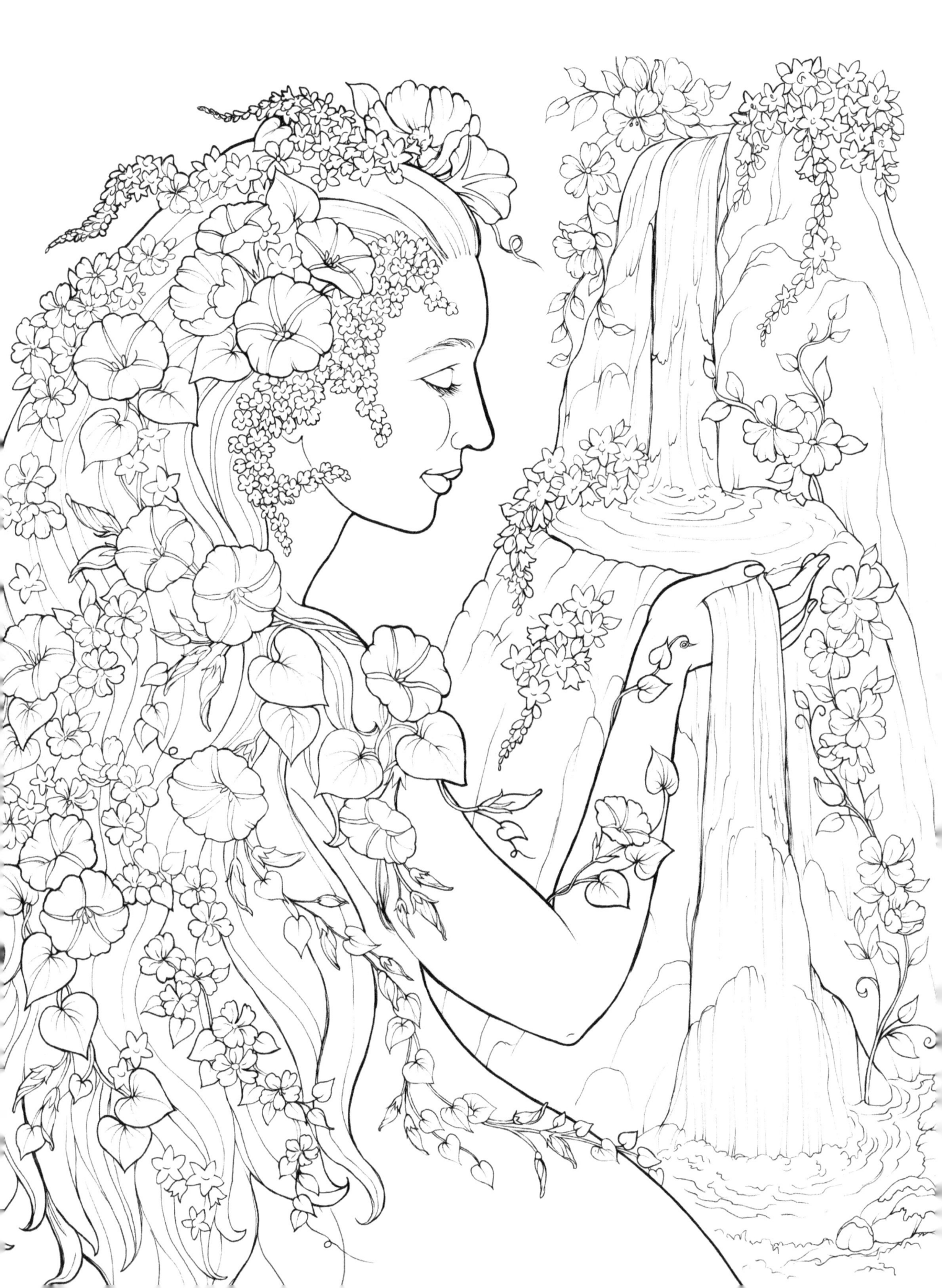

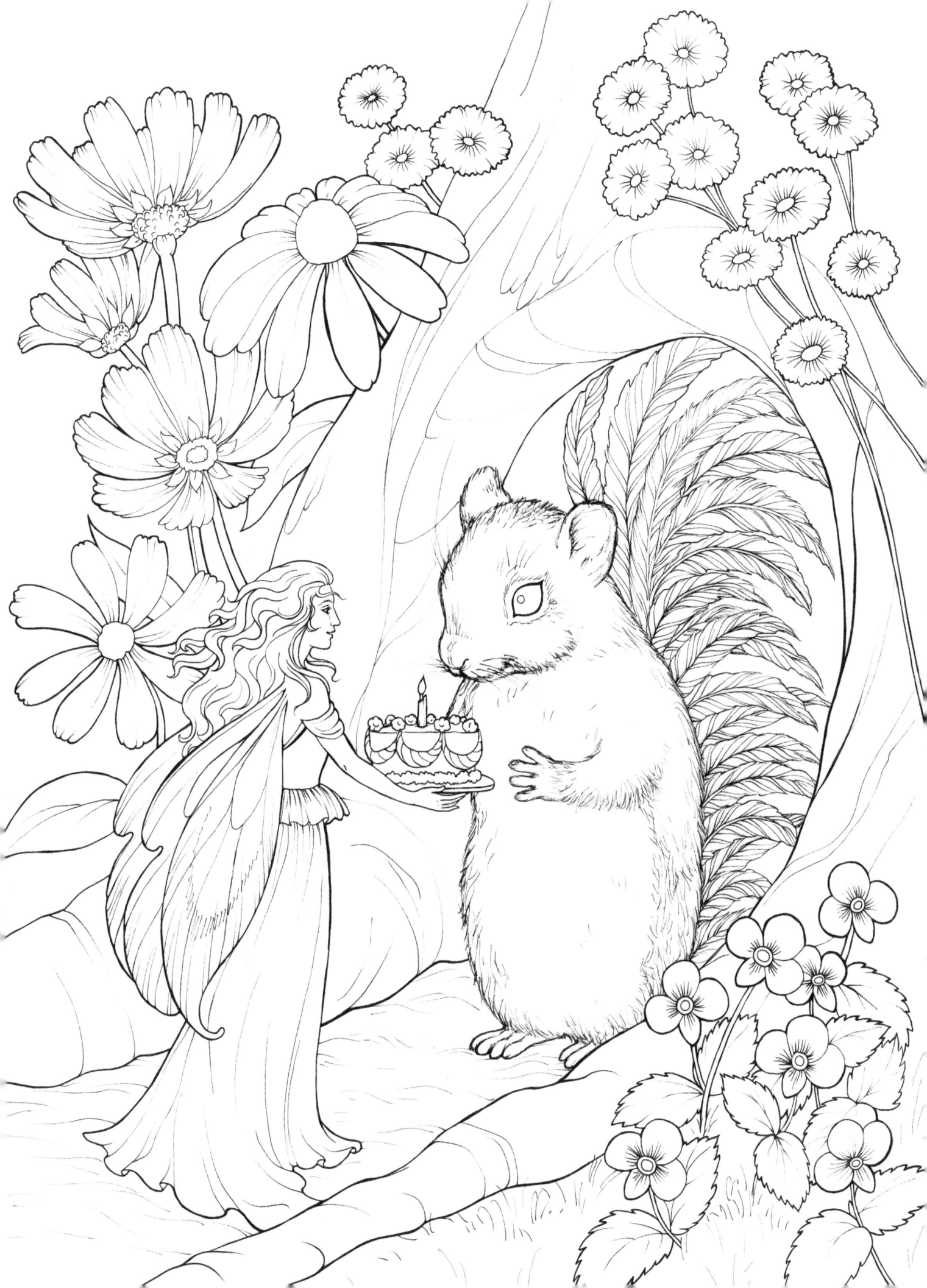

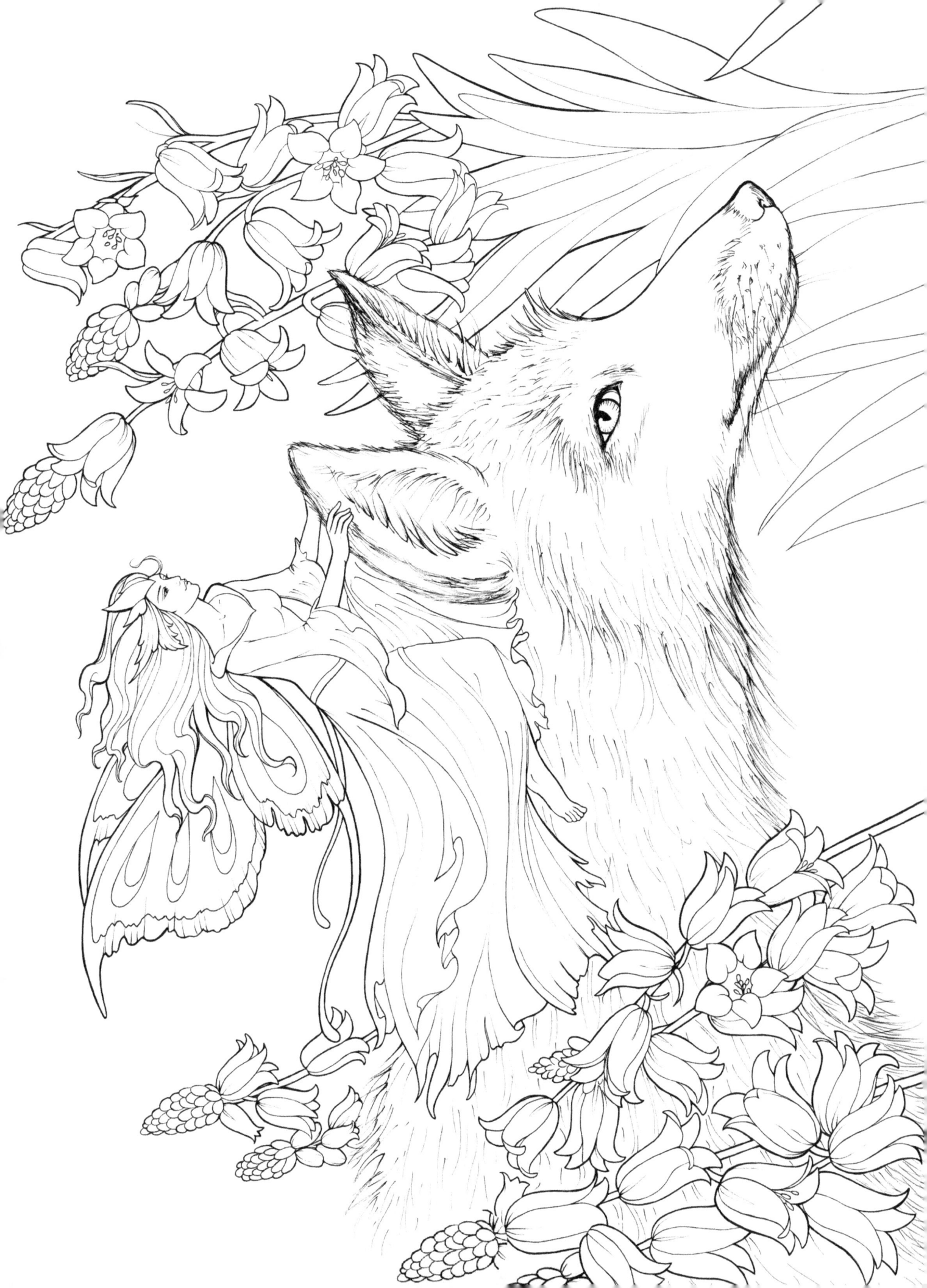

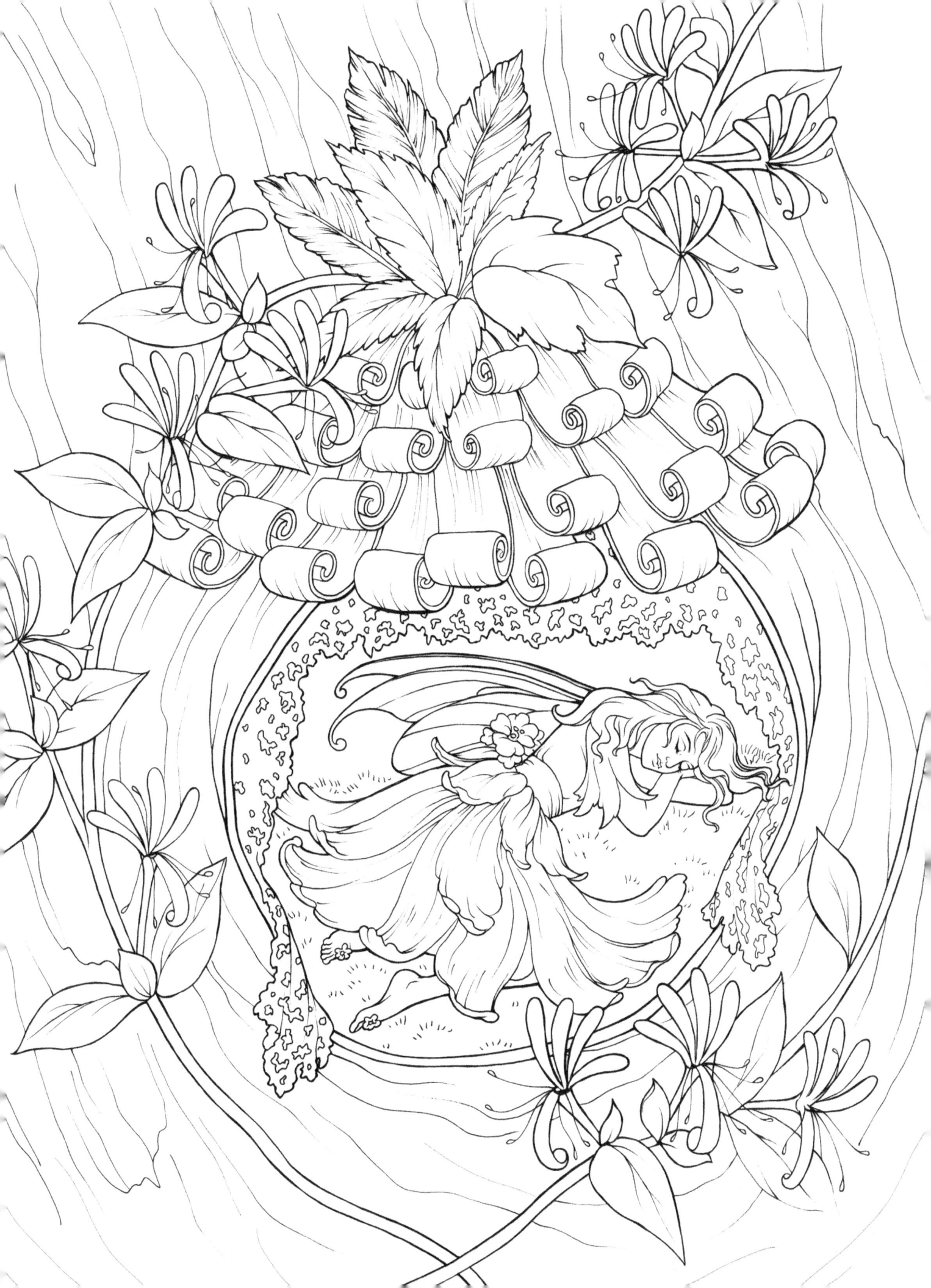

www.ingramcontent.com/pod-product-compliance
Lightning Source LLC
Chambersburg PA
CBHW080846170526
45158CB00009B/2649